The
Highway
of
Holiness

Olusola Osinoiki

The Highway of Holiness

A close look at holiness for this generation

Pleasant Word
A Division of WINEPRESS PUBLISHING

© 2008 by Olusola Osinoiki. All rights reserved.

Pleasant Word (a division of WinePress Publishing, PO Box 428, Enumclaw, WA 98022) functions only as book publisher. As such, the ultimate design, content, editorial accuracy, and views expressed or implied in this work are those of the author.

No part of this publication may be reproduced, stored in a retrieval system or transmitted in any way by any means—electronic, mechanical, photocopy, recording or otherwise—without the prior permission of the copyright holder, except as provided by USA copyright law.

Unless otherwise noted, all Scriptures are taken from the King James Version of the Bible.

Scripture quotations marked NIV are taken from the *Holy Bible, New International Version*®. NIV®. Copyright © 1973, 1978, 1984 by the International Bible Society. Used by permission of Zondervan. All rights reserved.

Scripture quotations marked AMP are taken from the Amplified Bible, Copyright © 1954, 1958, 1962, 1964, 1965, 1987 by The Lockman Foundation. Used by permission.

ISBN 13: 978-1-4141-1059-2
ISBN 10: 1-4141-1059-6
Library of Congress Catalog Card Number: 2007905331

Dedication

*To Christians in the nation of Mexico
as they wait on God for the transformation of their nation.*

Contents

Inspiration..ix
Foreword..xi
Why Another Book on Holiness?................................xiii
Acknowledgments xv
Introduction... xvii

Chapter 1: The State of the Human Race............................25

Chapter 2: Keys to Our Pursuit of Holiness 29
    1. *Faith* 29
    2. *A Thirst and Hunger for Holiness*................. 30
    3. *Consecration*... 31
    4. *Steadfastness*... 32

Chapter 3: Fruits of a Holy Life 35
    1. *Inner Victory and Freedom*............................ 35
    2. *Internal and External Holiness*...................... 36

   3. *Love for the Brethren* 37
   4. *Right Thoughts and Motives* 38
   5. *Unity in the Body of Christ* 39

Chapter 4: Maintaining a Holy Lifestyle 41
   1. *Fellowship with Other Believers* 41
   2. *Share Our Faith with Others* 42
   3. *Abide in the Truth* 43
   4. *Beware of Compromise* 44
   5. *Be Watchful and Prayerful* 46
   6. *Consecrate Our All to the Lord* 47
   7. *Avoid Foolish and Corrupt Conversations* 49

Conclusion 51

INSPIRATION

And an highway shall be there, and a way, and it shall be called the way of holiness; the unclean shall not pass over it; but it shall be for those: the wayfaring men, though fools, shall not err therein.

—Isaiah 35:8

Foreword

The Highway of Holiness is timely; it comes at a point when the Church seems to have forgotten about holiness and doesn't say anything about this subject anymore. These days, what we want to talk about and want to hear about is how to get rich quick, receive our miracles, or get our problems solved at the expense of living in sin.

Indeed, there is confusion out there! The values we used to hold dear in the '80s and early '90s have now been replaced by a flurry of get rich quick schemes—a mentality of "bring your money to church and don't worry about the fact that you stole it or duped somebody to get it. As long as you pay your tithe and give offerings, it's OK!"

Well, it's not OK! Holiness is not a very popular subject in this present day and age, but anyone who truly yearns for truth, fulfillment, peace of heart and mind and real prosperity will *dare* to read this book! *The Highway of Holiness* has broadened my knowledge, refreshed my devotion to God and renewed my passion and hunger for holiness.

I see a revival coming. It is my prayer that God will take *The Highway of Holiness* and use it to birth a fresh fire—a fire of desire to live holy lives and please God in obedience. I pray that everyone who reads *The Highway of Holiness* will, as I have, experience a new focus to live in the true essence of Christianity and teach others to do the same. May that fire spread to the nations and the uttermost parts of the earth. Amen.

Warning! This book may change your life!

Babalola Opeyemi Olusanya
TheProphetic Inc.

Why Another Book on Holiness?

There has been a lot written on this subject, but there is no one book that can really explain it all. I believe this book is just another signpost on the Highway of Holiness that will encourage us to continue on the journey of life in pursuit of a life like Christ's. This book's core concept focuses on holiness as a result of Christ's finished work. Hopefully, I will be able to take a complex topic and present it in a simple way.

Acknowledgments

First, thanks be to God, the author of life, the creator of all things, who gives us all things to enjoy. I would also like to thank my darling wife, Morunkunbi Osinoiki, for her support and editing work on this project. Thanks to my children Olumide, Olamide and Oyinlola for their support. I love you all very much.

A big thanks to all members of God's Battle Axe Fellowship, Agbor, Delta State, Nigeria, where I learned the importance of holiness. Thanks to you for making my National Youth Service a learning experience. Thanks to all at Runnymede Christian Fellowship, Egham, who stand shoulder to shoulder with me.

Many thanks to Julia Food, Kevin and Rosie Lewis, Kola Tayo and Angela Nnaji for time spent proofreading the manuscript of this book. My thanks also to Ope Olusanya for writing the Foreword.

Finally, my thanks to everyone for taking the time to read this book. May the entrance of God's word bring light to your path.

Olusola Osinoiki
Josh Publications

Introduction

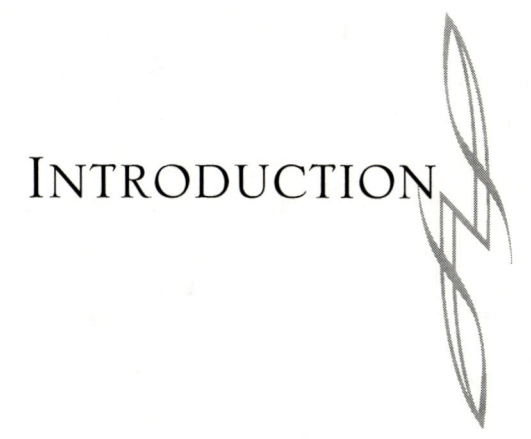

What is holiness? This question, I am sure, has flashed through the minds of a lot of people in and out of the Church. English dictionaries define "holiness" as sanctity, a state of being holy. "Sanctity" is sacredness or inviolability. "Sacred" means to be dedicated, regarded as holy, set apart and reserved. "Inviolable" means to be sacred, not to be profaned. To be holy is thus to be morally and spiritually excellent or perfect and to be revered. A holy thing is a devoted thing belonging to God and empowered by God.

From a biblical point of view, we can define holiness as a state of being pure, being good and being loved by God. Holiness means being set apart for something that is dedicated. Holiness did not spring up in the days of the New Testament apostles; it has been around since the foundations of the earth. Holiness is like an ancient landmark to God's people that was established from the foundations of the earth.

Holiness was a condition that Moses had to fulfill before he could talk to God. When Moses had his encounter with God in Exodus 3:5, he took off his sandals in obedience to God's command. God was manifesting Himself to Moses. God was there, and the ground itself was made holy. Holiness was a doctrine maintained through the dispensation of the Law; was pronounced and observed through the times of the judges, kings and prophets in the Old Testament; was taught by Jesus Christ (see Matthew 5:8,48) and was upheld by the apostles (see Hebrews 12:14). Therefore, no government, politician, prophet, religious leader, scientist, theologian, lawmaker, occultist, spiritualist, demon, fortune-teller or anyone else can abolish it. It is an absolute truth that no one can abolish holiness, because it is our only means of seeing God.

The writer of Hebrews has an encouraging and challenging word for us:

> Follow peace with all men, and holiness, without which no man shall see the Lord.
>
> (Hebrews 12:14)

> Make every effort to live in peace with all men and to be holy; without holiness no one will see the Lord.
>
> (NIV)

> Strive to live in peace with everybody and pursue that consecration and holiness without which no one will [ever] see the Lord.
>
> (AMP)

Because holiness is such a fundamental ingredient of our walk with God, the writer of Hebrews says that without it we shall not be able to see God. Moses took off his sandals in acknowledgement of God's holiness. Moses' obedience granted him access to God. I thank God that we don't have to take off our sandals as he did—all we have to do is let Jesus into our hearts and the process can begin.

Jesus' blood makes us pure; His blood gives us access to His righteousness. Every human being was born with an Adamic nature. We were born in sin, but as we accept all that Jesus did for us on the cross, we are freed from that Adamic nature.

> Wherefore, as by one man sin entered into the world and death by sin; and so death passed upon all men, for that all have sinned: (For until the law sin was in the world: but sin is not imputed when there is no law.) Nevertheless death reigned from Adam to Moses, even over them that had not sinned after the similitude of Adam's transgression, who is the figure of him that was to come.
> (Romans 5:12-14)

It is clear from the above scripture that the sinful nature is passed down as an inheritance to us as individuals. If we as individuals therefore refuse to accept the gift offered to us in Jesus Christ, we will continue in sin. In Job 14:4, Job brings clarity to this with the statement, "Who can bring a clean thing out of an unclean? Not one." It is very true that we can't make ourselves clean and acceptable before God. Only God through Christ can make individuals born in sin acceptable to Him.

How can we who are born of this world be made clean? Psalm 51:5 declares that we were born in sin. Paul makes this clear in Romans when he writes, "All have sinned" (3:23). We need to know in our hearts and in our minds that there is no one who is holy before God without Christ. The devil would like us to believe that we can be holy without God, but this is simply not true. The holiness we receive is as a result of yielding and accepting Christ's sacrifice. It is only through Christ and in Christ that we can wipe away the works of the flesh in our lives. In Galatians 5:19-21, Paul the apostle reveals to us the works of the flesh that we must yield to God in order to be dead to them. These works of the flesh put us into bondage; Christ's death makes us free.

> Knowing this, that our old man is crucified with him, that the body of sin might be destroyed, that henceforth we should not serve sin.
>
> (Romans 6:6)

When Jesus died on the cross, He crucified our old man there—the man of sin in which we were born. Sin stops us from getting to heaven. Heaven is the dwelling place of God and is where the throne of God is. God the Father dwells in heaven (see Matthew 5:16,45; 6:9,10; 7:11,21). Jesus came from there, went there and will come back from there (see Acts 1:9-11). Heaven is our home as well. Jesus said that He was going there to prepare a place for us (see John 14:2-3). Yet God is a holy God, so before we can go before Him, we must be holy, too.

> Who shall ascend into the hill of the LORD? Or who shall stand in his holy place? He that hath clean hands, and a

pure heart; who hath not lifted up his soul unto vanity, nor sworn deceitfully.

(Psalm 24:3-4)

Follow peace with all men, and holiness, without which no man shall see the Lord.

(Hebrews 12:14)

It is very clear from the scriptures above that if we are not holy, we cannot see God. In our own strength, we can't overcome sin. We need the blood of Jesus to cleanse, uproot and amputate the roots of sin in our lives.

As we look at the requirement of holiness for God's children, let us bear in mind that being holy is a requirement that God sets for all His people.

Sanctify yourselves therefore, and be ye holy: for I am the LORD your God.

(Leviticus 20:7)

But as he which hath called you is holy, so be ye holy in all manner of conversation.

(1 Peter 1:15)

When God called Abraham to serve him, He commanded him to be perfect (see Genesis 17:1). This perfection relates to a blameless life, a life without blemish, a holy life. God required from Abraham a holy and perfect lifestyle. Holiness is really about completeness, wholeness and soundness—a heart that is undivided in its devotion to God. In Matthew 5:48, Jesus encourages us to be perfect just as our Father is perfect. God has said on many occasions throughout scripture that we should be holy (see Exodus 22:31; Leviticus 11:44; 20:26; 2 Peter 3:11).

One note of warning here: we are no more under the Law but under grace. Under the Law we were told what to eat and drink, and there was clear punishment for disobedience on earth. Under grace we still have to comply with God's Law, but we do that through Christ.

I have spoken about Christ's death earlier; His death brings us a right standing with God (righteousness). Therefore, under grace God cleanses even the things we eat, just as He did for Peter. In Acts 10:11-15, God presented to Peter a selection of food that under the Law was unholy but through Christ's death and resurrection had been made holy. Likewise, in God's sight, the Gentiles, being not born of the lineage of Abraham, were an unholy people before Him. However, they can now become God's holy people, through Christ, because His death purifies them.

To sanctify is to make holy. In Numbers 11:18, as in other parts of Scripture, the Lord encourages us to sanctify ourselves. In 1 Chronicles 15:11-13, before the priests could touch the Ark of the Covenant (the dwelling place of God's presence in the Old Testament within the Tabernacle and the first Temple), they were required to sanctify themselves. In John 17:17, Jesus makes us aware that we are sanctified by the Word of God. Hebrews 13:12 tells us that we are sanctified by Jesus' blood. As I said before, under grace, Christ assists us in the process of sanctification. Christ would not be helping us to be holy if it were an unnecessary requirement.

Another reason why we must take this call to holiness seriously is because our Father is a holy God. The holiness of God is essential to His nature and emphasizes His divine perfection. Our God is holy, and all through Scripture this is declared (see Leviticus 19:2; 21:8, Joshua 24:19; 1 Samuel 2:2; Psalm 99:5; Isaiah 5:16; Hosea 11:9; Revelation 4:8). We are also told in Habakkuk 2:20 that God's house, His Temple, is considered holy. The book of Psalms makes the same statement in Psalm 5:7. God is also called the Holy One of Israel (see Psalm 71:22; 78:41; 89:18; Jeremiah 51:5; Ezekiel 39:7). Even the heavenly beings know that God is holy (see Revelation 4:8). We are declared to be the children of God, offspring of the Almighty. If we are children of God and God is holy, then we are to be holy children and to remain holy children.

CHAPTER 1

THE STATE OF THE HUMAN RACE

As we look at the world, there is a clear sense of the earth being full of both holy and unholy people. Each human being was at one point unholy; the Bible says we were born in sin. Leviticus 10:10 leads us to understand that there is a clear distinction between the holy and the unholy. Christ is the only way in which the human race can progress from unholiness to holiness. Which side are we on?

God has the ability to transform our unholy lives into holy ones if we allow Him. In Hebrews 10:10, we see that we are made holy because of the offering of the body of the Lord. Jesus' death and suffering was God's way of sanctifying the human race (see Hebrews 13:12). God has a mission to sanctify this human race unto Himself. God is holy, and He wants our lives to conform to His holiness. Jesus pleaded with the Father in John 17:17 that we should be made holy through God's word.

Our God, the God of Peace (Jehovah Shalom), is willing to make us holy in spirit, soul and body. This process of purification enables us to be used by a holy God. As long as we are willing, the Lord is willing.

> Abstain from all appearance of evil. And the very God of peace sanctify you wholly; and I pray God your whole spirit and soul and body be preserved blameless unto the coming of our Lord Jesus Christ.
> (1 Thessalonians 5:22-23)

In 1 Thessalonians 5:22, Paul encourages us to refrain from all appearances of evil. We, as children of God, should flee from anything that has even a vague resemblance to evil. Our love for God should restrain us from evil. As we abstain from evil, He makes a commitment to sanctify us and make us holy. In 2 Timothy 2:19-21, Paul places a strong emphasis on us being vessels of honor, which comes as a result of us purging ourselves and refraining from evil. True holiness is when our whole being—spirit, soul and body—is in peace and harmony in the will of God.

Let us look at another scripture from Paul's first letter to the Thessalonians.

> For this is the will of God, even your sanctification, that ye should abstain from fornication.
> (1 Thessalonians 4:3)

It is clear that the Lord wants us to live a pure and holy life. The key point to remember when we look at the human race and the Church is that God has the ability and the desire to purify the human race by His word. God can make us a holy people unto Himself if we yield in obedience to Him. A life of purity comes as we determine in our own lives, by the grace of God and through the finished work of the cross, to think differently than the original sinful nature into which we were all born. We must make a determined decision to flee all appearances of evil. God requires us to repent from our old ways of disobedience and live a life of obedience.

Repentance involves a decision to turn away from one course and turn toward another. As we turn away from a life of sin to a life that stems from the sacrifice of Jesus on the cross, His blood has enough power to make us (the entire human race) wholly sanctified.

How do we accept what Christ did on the cross for us? It is quite simple: it starts at the point of repentance. We have to acknowledge that we need to repent of our old ways, knowing that our own ways are not pure before God. God is holy and His ways are pure, so as we yield to Him, He makes us pure. The entire human race is impure because of Adam and Eve's sin in the Garden of Eden, but through the death of Christ, we can become pure. Our sanctification is the will of God, and through the death of Jesus, not laws and rules, we have been given access to God.

Accepting Christ is therefore the starting point on our journey along this Highway of Holiness. The question then becomes, *How can we continually pursue holiness?* We know that without it, we can't see God (see Hebrews 12:14). Life in Christ does not free us from the temptations of this life. Therefore, as a people we must be in continual pursuit of a holy life. Just like a marathon runner who pursues the final goal in earnest because he knows that ultimately he will obtain the prize, we too must pursue our prize: eternal life with God.

CHAPTER 2
Keys to Our Pursuit of Holiness

In this chapter, we will look at four keys to help us in pursuit of holiness. These keys are essential to enable us to live a holy life in the sight of God.

1. Faith

We need to believe that we can be made holy. When we look at our imperfect world, we may have a tendency to think that having a life of holiness is impossible. However, we need to believe that being holy is something we can pursue. If we do not start from this basic principle, our pursuit of holiness is flawed. We must believe that we can conform to the divine nature of God. Just as we were once conformed to the standards of this world that are opposed to God, we must now believe that we can be conformed to God's standard. This sense of assurance does not come from our works but from the finished work of Christ.

Mary, the mother of Jesus, was told in Luke 1:45 that if she believed, the promises spoken to her would be fulfilled. Likewise, we need to believe that God's desire is to make us holy and that if we believe this we can align ourselves with God's will and live a holy life. We should not desire holiness in order to appear superior to others; rather, we should pursue holiness out of a desire to be closer to God.

There is an element of faith that is needed to continue on this road of holiness. If we have faith and believe the plans and purposes of God, we will live lives that please God. When Paul was in the boat in Acts 27:25, he told his companions on the ship to be happy because he believed that everything told to him would be fulfilled as promised. This came to pass because he believed. We must likewise just believe that God wants to make us holy.

2. A Thirst and Hunger for Holiness

If we desire something from our earthly fathers, they are likely to give it to us based on our need and eager desire for it. It is the same with God. If we eagerly desire to live a holy life under God and hunger and thirst for it, God will grant us the desires of our heart. If we are hungry, a drink can't quench our hunger. We are only filled when we eat food. In the same way, our spiritual man desires to conform to the image of God and is hungry for the nature of God's holiness. It can only be fulfilled when it encounters the nature of God.

As believers, we often look at the imperfections around us and see men and women of God falling from grace with one sin or another. We tend to limit ourselves to their failures or successes. Great men and women of God are there as examples, but they should not be our yardstick. They are just pointers on the highway and should motivate us to continually pursue holiness.

Often, we see people not attaining a higher level of holiness in their personal walk with God because of wrong teaching, unbelief, laziness and lack of commitment. As stated before, pursuing holiness is directly related to how much we want to change and be better aligned with the Holy One. Our pastors and other leaders are not the yardsticks we should measure our lives by. We need to set our goals on the one who died on the cross for us all—Jesus. We need to have a hunger and a thirst to be conformed to His image: a life that knew no sin, yet carried the sins of the world.

3. Consecration

"Consecration" means to set oneself aside for service to God. If we have a true desire to be set apart for God and live our lives in line with that desire, we will see ourselves living holier lives. It starts with a determination in our hearts that we are going to give our lives over to God and is only completed when we commit to the journey. As we give ourselves to God, God delights in us and helps us through His Holy Spirit.

In Psalm 73:25, the psalmist says, "Whom have I in heaven but thee? and there is none upon earth that I desire beside thee." This is the same level of commitment we must have toward God—a strong desire to see Him, to serve Him, and to walk with Him. The psalmist's words fit nicely with Paul's words in his second letter to Timothy where he talks about vessels of honor and dishonor. The key to being a vessel of honor—a vessel consecrated to the Most High—is to purge oneself (see 2 Timothy 2:21). We have to have a strong determination in our hearts to serve God. Like the deer pants for water, so must our desire be for Him.

If we make up our minds to be undistracted and undiverted, we will be able to focus on Him in the midst of a busy life. We just have to make the choice to pursue the holiness of God. As we pursue this holiness, we will further develop our relationship with a holy God.

4. Steadfastness

To be "steadfast" is to be fixed, firm and unyielding. We need to be focused on the objective that is set before us as believers, to be all that God desires us to be. In our pursuit of a holy God and a holy life, we need to be steadfast. James gives us a good picture that we can use to relate to a steadfast heart.

> But let him ask in faith, nothing wavering. For he that wavereth is like a wave of the sea driven with the wind and tossed. For let not that man think that he shall receive any thing of the Lord. A double minded man is unstable in all his ways.
>
> (James 1:6-8)

In this passage, James encourages us to ask in faith, not doubting in our hearts, and to be steadfast with an assurance that it is the Father's good pleasure to make us more like Him in every way. We are partakers of Christ's nature. Christ was pure; He offers us total deliverance from inner sin and promises a life of purity and peace in Him. This is the promise of God. We can therefore be steadfast in our requests to Him.

There is a beautiful story in the Bible in which Jacob wrestles with God. The place he wrestled with God day and night is called

Peniel (see Genesis 32:24-30). The verse that gets my attention is verse 26: "And he said, Let me go, for the day breaketh. And he said, I will not let thee go, except thou bless me." Here, we see Jacob being steadfast in his request. This is a good example of how we should be unwavering in our request for a holy life that can only come through our relationship and fellowship with the Lord. We can place demands on God's grace for Him to purify us and show us areas in our life that need to be changed.

To obtain true holiness, we need to pursue God. In our pursuit of Him, we become more like Him. The foundation for this pursuit is Christ. As we confess our sins to Him, He is faithful to forgive us because He loves us. He desires that, like the woman caught in adultery, we receive His forgiveness and sin no more.

If you have never asked the Lord to come into your life and be your Lord and personal Savior, but want to get on this Highway of Holiness, now is a good time to ask Him in. Just confess your sins to Him. Tell Jesus that you recognize you are a sinner born in sin, ask Him to forgive you your sins, and then promise by His strength in you to depart from evil. Accept Him as your Lord. Ask Him to make you holy—He will. If you have just prayed that prayer for the first time, be assured that Christ acknowledges you and that you are His child. His Spirit is upon you, and you are His.

Christ has a plan that His church would be a holy church. Look at what Paul says in the passage below:

> That he might sanctify and cleanse it with the washing of water by the word, That he might present it to himself a

glorious church, not having spot, or wrinkle, or any such thing; but that it should be holy and without blemish.

(Ephesians 5:26-27)

We can base our hunger for holiness and our steadfast desire for holiness on this scriptural truth. Christ wants us to be holy; it is His desire. Again, in Philippians 2:15, we see Christ's desire. Even in a crooked world, God still wants us to be a holy people. When God examines a holy heart, He finds all that it possesses to be in harmony with Him—a throne on which He can reign without a rival, where He can exercise undisputed domination. That is why we must consecrate ourselves to Him.

To conclude this chapter, let me just say to you that a holy life is not possible without the Holy Spirit. The Holy Spirit is the comforter that Jesus promised us. Jesus said that the Holy Spirit would lead us into all truth (see John 16:13). Jesus told His disciples to receive the Holy Spirit; we are Christ's followers, so we must also receive the promise of the Holy Spirit. On the Highway of Holiness, our only true helper who keeps us on track is the Holy Spirit. The Bible says that "as many are led by the Spirit, they are the children of God" (Romans 8:14). Our Father is holy, and if we yield to the Holy Spirit, we shall be holy too.

CHAPTER 3
FRUITS OF A HOLY LIFE

As we truly pursue holiness in our walk with God, we show forth the fruits of a life transformed. These fruits are evidence that a change has truly taken place inside us. Jesus said in Matthew 7:18 that a good tree can only bring forth good fruit, while a bad tree can bring forth only bad fruit. If we are truly walking in obedience to the Lord's command to be holy, we will manifest the fruits of holiness in our day-to-day lives—at school, in the office, on the bus, in church and basically anywhere. In this chapter, we will look at five key fruits in the life of a believer that has been made holy by Christ and is continuing in the pursuit of holiness.

1. Inner Victory and Freedom

As we live lives of holiness, we begin to sense a great freedom and peace in our communication with God. This peace quickly transforms into rest (see Hebrews 4:9) and a sense of victory, no matter what the external circumstances present to us. In

Ephesians 2:7, Paul speaks of the promise of God's kindness to God's people. Having a holy walk in Christ enables us to approach God with boldness; we are not afraid of God because His life is in our lives.

If we abide in Christ, we abide in the truth of His word. The Bible says we should know the truth and that the truth sets us free (see John 8:36). We find a new freedom in ourselves as we align ourselves to the truth of God's Word about our need to be holy. The enemy constantly fights to get us to a place of anxiety and discomfort, but if our lives reflect the life of God, we will be encompassed by God's sweet presence.

God is holy, and we take on His character and nature as we spend time with Him. The greatest victory we have in Christ is to know that the Lord is on our side and that He is our defense. Joshua understood this quite clearly when he met the Lord before the battle of Jericho. He left God's holy presence with an assurance of victory, because he knew that the Lord was on his side (see Joshua 5:13-15). We can know that same level of victory on the inside before the external battle is won, based on our commitment to live a holy life.

2. Internal and External Holiness

Our holiness is sourced from within, which means that if our hearts are totally taken over by Christ as a result of His work on Calvary, there should be a reflection of this in our outer man. Our outer man is what those in the world around us see. They see our character, our manners, our expressions and our behaviors, which are the result of the inner working of Christ in our lives. When people look at us, we are to be the reflection of Christ in every way. Our light must so shine that all see our good works and glorify God. The source of a holy life is a holy heart. We have a new way of living; we now have the grace to have a holy lifestyle.

The Holy Spirit has His home in our hearts. The Bible describes the Holy Spirit as our guide and states that those led by the Holy Spirit are the children of God (see Romans 8:14). The Holy Spirit leads us to this holy lifestyle; the Holy Spirit within us is at war with sin and disobedience. If the Spirit truly leads, then the life we live will reflect the character of a holy God.

We know that we are not saved by our own works. However, as a result of having a holy lifestyle, the works we do are good works. In Titus 2:14, Paul reveals this as part of God's plan for our lives: "Who gave himself for us, that he might redeem us from all iniquity, and purify unto himself a peculiar people, zealous of good works." Jesus redeemed us so that we might do good works. These good works come as a result of the holy lifestyle we live as we embrace the cross. Look at the above scripture again. God redeemed us from unholiness and made us holy in order that we might do good works. What an amazing plan of redemption.

> A good man out of the good treasure of the heart bringeth forth good things: and an evil man out of the evil treasure bringeth forth evil things.
>
> (Matthew 12:35)

3. Love for the Brethren

> For, brethren, ye have been called unto liberty; only use not liberty for an occasion to the flesh, but by love serve one another.
>
> (Galatians 5:13)

As stated already, our holy lifestyle is a result of Christ's work. Jesus gave us two commandments while He was on earth that sum up the Ten Commandments. The first is to love God. Out of that love for God, we should desire to be like Him and have a holy lifestyle. The second commandment Jesus gave us is to love our neighbors as ourselves (see Matthew 22:37-40). In Galatians 5:13, Paul expresses the same thought. We are called to liberty in Christ—freedom from the consequences of sin—as we live in obedience to Him. True proof of this liberty and freedom is that we walk in love. Jesus is our perfect example. He was a holy sacrifice and laid down His life for all in love (see John 3:16).

Our love and commitment to God should be the key to our loving others. Holiness is part of God's nature; love is also part of His nature. The evidence that we have a holy lifestyle is that we walk in love. The *Amplified Version* of 1 Peter 1:22 gives us an even clearer understanding of this:

> Since by your obedience to the Truth through the Holy Spirit you have purified your hearts for the sincere affection of the brethren, [see that you] love one another fervently from a pure heart.

4. Right Thoughts and Motives

In Galatians 5:16-18, the apostle Paul encourages us to walk in the Spirit and not in the flesh. If we obey this injunction, we will have the fruit in the outworking of a holy life. As we yield to the Spirit, we give ourselves the space to have right motives. If we have unholy thoughts, they will express themselves in an unholy lifestyle. On the other hand, if we live a life of holiness, we will have right and pure motives because we are yielded to the Lord.

Right thoughts born out of a holy life are the key to having the right motives. As people of God, we should not try in our own strength to have right thoughts, because our efforts are not good enough. We need God to help us in order to have a truly righteous basis for our thoughts, motives and actions.

Having the right thoughts and motives in the world in which we live is an essential fruit of a holy life. True holiness produces fruit, not just in the Church, but also as we go about our daily lives. This fruit is a powerful key to righteousness in any nation.

5. Unity in the Body of Christ

The Bible says that Christ is holy and that those who are made holy shall be in unity because they are all holy (see Hebrews 2:11). Holy living is one of the keys to unity among Christians and is also the evidence of that unity. Christ is holy and makes us holy; hence, we have common ground. It is therefore necessary for us to continue to live holy lives to ensure the unity of the saints.

Scripture encourages us to keep the unity of the Spirit (see Ephesians 4:3). We have to work at this. We have to work at living a holy life, but when we with the help of the Holy Spirit succeed, the result is unity. The person who leads an unholy life has the ingredients for division in their life: backbiting, gossiping, lying, cheating and jealousy. These are all fruits of an unholy life, and they foster division.

> Now I beseech you, brethren, by the name of our Lord Jesus Christ, that ye all speak the same thing and there be no divisions among you; but that ye be perfectly joined together in the same mind and in the same judgment.
>
> (1 Corinthians 1:10)

The Bible says that out of the abundance of the heart the mouth speaks (see Matthew 12:34), so we need to guard our hearts. The best way to guard our hearts is to seek God and obey His Word. As we obey His Word to live a holy life, we begin to think the right thoughts and speak forth the right things. As Paul shows us in 1 Corinthians 1:10 above, if we speak the same thing, there will be no divisions. This can only be achieved if we yield to the Holy One who makes us holy. Psalm 133 also reveals that it is a good thing for brethren to dwell together in unity. God desires this.

Now that we have a clear understanding about living a holy life and know some of the fruits of a holy life, we can see the connection between our salvation and a life of holiness. We now need to have an idea of how to maintain a holy life. Just as an engineer who builds a car gives the buyer of the car a handbook on how to maintain the car, we as believers, made holy by the work of Jesus on Calvary, need to follow God's Word to maintain a holy life. In the last chapter of this book, I will share some principles that will help us maintain holiness in our day-to-day lives.

CHAPTER 4

Maintaining a Holy Lifestyle

Unless we are vigilant, watchful and prayerful, the enemy will rob us of the peace that comes with a holy lifestyle. We want to progress forward on this Highway of Holiness toward the high calling in Christ—our home in His heavenly kingdom. We are in a battle. The enemy, the devil, does not want us to be together with the One who makes us holy. The devil does not want us to fulfill the purposes of God, but almighty God does want us to do His will while we are on the earth. God knows that we have to live holy lives as Christians, and He has given us guidelines through His Word to help us.

1. Fellowship with Other Believers

One of the ways to maintain a lifestyle of holiness is to have regular fellowship with other believers. One of the rewards of fellowship is the opportunity to hear other people's experience of their walk with God. As we learn, we give ourselves capacity to grow. In the book of Acts, we see that the believers gathered together regularly (see Acts 2:1,44). In Colossians 3:16, Paul states that when we come together and one has a psalm, one has a word and another has a song, all these can help us to encourage one another. In Hebrews 10:25, we are encouraged to meet together. Jesus said that where two or three are gathered together, He would be there in the midst of His people (see Matthew 18:20).

There is an enormous amount of enrichment that a believer experiences when God's people are gathered together. Being a member of a group of believers can be a great encouragement to us, because it helps us with accountability and ultimately helps us with our walk with God. True holiness means we can walk in love, and as we walk in love with one another, our lives conform to the image of Christ more and more. Holiness comes to us as a result of Christ's sacrifice on the cross. The best expression of holiness is seen in His life.

2. Share Our Faith with Others

In John 1, Andrew told Peter that he had found the Messiah. This gave Peter the opportunity to meet Jesus, after which time he decided to follow Him. The life of Andrew was full of similar incidents in which he introduced people to Jesus (see John 2:21-22; 6:8-9). The Lord has committed the same task into our hands. We are all called to the ministry of reconciling others to Christ.

Philip, like Andrew, was always telling people about Jesus. In Acts 8:38, we read, "And he commanded the chariot to stand still: and they went down both into the water, both Philip and the eunuch; and he baptized him." If our Christianity is worth having, then it is truly worthy sharing. Disciples are to be examples of what they preach. As we live for Christ in true holiness, our lives should speak as living epistles. We are followers of Jesus, and He is our leader and our head. We follow Him, and as we find freedom in Him, we ought to share it.

Throughout Jesus' life, He spoke constantly of His heavenly Father. Toward the end of His life, He spoke of the Holy Spirit. We are to speak of Jesus, His love, His grace and His mercy to all men. As we commit to living a life of being a witness for Christ, we, of necessity, must commit at the same time to a life of holiness.

3. Abide in the Truth

Once we discover the truth of God's Word, we must abide in it. We must meditate on it. Jesus said that the words He spoke were both spirit and life and that they would set us free. Galatians 3:1 reveals that the church in Galatia was wandering away from the truth. Paul encouraged them to remember Jesus, in whom their salvation was rooted. Likewise, we need to be stable and rooted in the Word of God, for the Word of God teaches us, encourages us and equips us for our walk on the Highway of Holiness. Jesus is that Word; John declared that the Word became flesh for us (see John 1:14).

As Joshua stepped into destiny and the challenge to take the Israelites into the Promised Land, he was encouraged to abide in the word.

> This book of the law shall not depart out of thy mouth; but thou shalt meditate therein day and night, that thou mayest observe to do according to all that is written therein: for then

thou shalt make thy way prosperous, and then thou shalt have good success.

(Joshua 1:8)

As we abide in the Word, we learn of the Word and are changed and challenged. Abraham gave heed to the word of God, and Paul in the book of Galatians says that it was counted to him for righteousness (see Galatians 3:6-9). The journey we embark on in life is full of temptations, victories over sin, trials, opportunities, disappointments and successes. This is the story of life, but as we abide in the Word of God, we find grace to stay focused and remain faithful to the course set before us: a life of holiness. God's word is a lamp to our feet, a light to our pathway and the food that supports our spirit and renews our soul.

4. Beware of Compromise

Compromise is an agreement in an argument in which the people involved reduce their demands or change their opinion in order to agree. We are to stand for the truth every day and in every way. Jesus stood for the purposes of His Father; He never compromised and was committed to the will of His Father. We are called by God to live for Him, and so we, too, must not compromise.

It is so easy to compromise our faith in the world that we live in. The enemy, peer pressure and the changing world all try to make us unfaithful to the truth of God's Word. People around us may compromise and be untruthful, but that is no excuse for us to do so. As true believers, we must stand for what we believe. God's Word says it is a sin to steal; we therefore must have the courage to obey—whether it be stealing from our parents, stealing from a friend, taking things from work or claiming time we didn't spend at work in our timesheets. Men and women who are dedicated to a lifestyle of holiness have no issues with these things. We as believers are not to go the way of the world. We must commit to what we believe and stand firm. The wind will blow, but we must be confident in the ability and grace of God to keep us strong on His Highway of Holiness if we truly let Him.

We are in the world, but not of this world. We are to be a light in the darkness. If we live a life of compromise, it will be difficult for us to shine as light. I am sure you have heard the saying "the pot calling the kettle black." This phrase is similar to the words of Jesus when He said we should remove the log in our own eyes before we attempt to remove the speck in some else's eyes (see Matthew 7:5). We should be aware of the trap of compromise. Young people who trust the Lord to live a holy life have temptation all around them. They need to say to themselves that being a virgin is worth a lot more than a night of sin. These are decisions that believers have to make on a daily basis. We must resist the temptations around us and not compromise.

Avoiding compromise in our lives is very personal. I could list a number of things that we should not do as Christians, but that would just be a list. As believers, we must yield to the Holy Spirit and let God show us the areas of compromise that present themselves and how we are to handle them. The reality is that compromise leads to sin, and sin is a hindrance to our walk on the highway of holiness. So beware of compromise; be true to the truth of God.

The Holy Spirit of God is our helper and our guide. He leads us into all truth. We should yield to the Spirit and allow Him to guide us on the pathway of life. God gave us His Spirit so that we can live the holy life He desires us to live. It is only as we are led by the Spirit of God that we can live above the fear of man, the love of pleasure, the lust of the flesh and the fear of failure, which are some of the common causes of compromise.

5. Be Watchful and Prayerful

Jesus lived as a man on the earth, and when He departed from the earth He gave us some sound advice. He said we should be as wise as a serpent and we should watch and pray. As believers, we have an enemy who wants to trip us up. The Bible says he goes about like a roaring lion looking for something to devour. The enemy, the devil, is dangerous, and we need to be watchful and prayerful in our walk.

> Be sober, be vigilant; because your adversary the devil, as a roaring lion, walketh about, seeking whom he may devour: Whom resist steadfast in the faith, knowing that the same afflictions are accomplished in your brethren that are in the world. But the God of all grace, who hath called us unto his eternal glory by Christ Jesus, after that ye have suffered a little while, make you perfect, stablish, strengthen, settle you. To him be glory and dominion for ever and ever. Amen.
> (1 Peter 5:8-11)

In the passage above, Peter encourages us to be sober and vigilant. There is a need for us as believers to be aware of the need for prayer. A dialogue with God makes us aware of the spiritual dimensions around us. Jesus is at the Father's side making intercession for us. He knows what it means to be tempted, which is why He said that we should watch and pray.

On the Highway of Holiness, praying and being alert are the keys to maintaining our fellowship with the Lord.

Better is the end of a matter than the beginning (see Ecclesiastes 7:8). As we journey on this highway we must be careful, as there are diversions, speed bumps and potholes that can take us off course. In most major cities around the world there are bypasses that go right around the city. While traveling on these roads, if we miss our junction because we were not watchful, we might have to go on an unnecessary detour. Likewise, we must be watchful that we don't fall into temptation. We must be fervent in prayer, as prayer is the key to the heart of the Almighty. He desires to instruct us in the way we should go. We just need to call out, "Thou Son of David, have mercy upon me" (see Matthew 15:22).

The good thing about it all is that we are not watching and praying alone. The Holy Spirit is here to help us stay focused on the will of God. The Bible says that we don't know how to pray but that the Spirit helps us (see Romans 8:26). In the same way, we don't know how to stand and watch. We need the Holy Spirit to watch over us so that we don't watch in vain.

> Behold, I come quickly: hold that fast which thou hast, that no man take thy crown.
>
> (Revelation 3:11)

6. Consecrate Our All to the Lord

While I was in college, I remember visiting a friend of mine at his university accommodation. I had my briefcase and I left it on the edge of his bed. It was a busy room with people coming in and out of the room. My briefcase was placed where I felt a thief could easily pick it up and run off with it. As my friend and I chatted together, I watched my briefcase. It got to a stage in the conversation that I could no longer hear him because I was focused solely on the briefcase. At that point my friend said to me, "Where your treasure is, that is where your heart will be." How true were his words in that instance! My heart was on my briefcase, and because of this I could not listen to him with my full attention.

We need to let our hearts be fully focused on Jesus, because He is our true treasure. In Philippians 3:7-17, we see Paul address this very issue. Paul says that he counted those things he had lost as a result of his conversion a loss for Christ. He continued by saying that he had forsaken the laws of men that gave false righteousness, and that he thought it right to take on himself the life-giving sacrifice of Jesus, the true key to righteousness. He forsook all in order to know more clearly and more intimately Jesus the Son of God, His suffering, and the power of His resurrection (see Philippians 3:8-11).

Paul was not claiming to be perfect in himself; he was looking to be made perfect in Christ. He knew that one of the keys to a fulfilled life in Christ was to forget the things behind him and to focus on the things ahead of him that he had in Christ (see Philippians 3:11-17). Let us imitate Paul in this by forgetting the things behind us and pressing on to obtain the prize of the high calling of God in Christ Jesus. Let us focus on Jesus and live a life wholly consecrated to the Lord. Whether in school, at the office, on the bus, at home or even in church, let Jesus be the focus.

In Acts 2:45, the Bible tells us that the people of the Early Church sold what they had and shared it with the family of God. The point here is the focus of the heart. Our hearts should be sold out totally to the Lord so that we can give up anything in the pursuit of His glory.

7. Avoid Foolish and Corrupt Conversations

In his letter to the Ephesians, Paul encourages us to put away evil speaking (see Ephesians 4:30-32). We might not realize it, but our thoughts and secrets are known by God and shall be judged as revealed in Matthew 15:19-20 and Romans 2:16. Therefore, we must be careful in what we say, do and think. God loves us very much, but He still desires that we live holy and pure lives.

As I come to the end of this book, there is one thing of which I am totally convinced: the Lord Himself is committed to helping us on this Highway of Holiness. If we cultivate a good habit of watching what we say, we shall have nothing to be ashamed of when we stand before Him on the day of glory.

> And that ye study to be quiet, and to do your own business, and to work with your own hands, as we commanded you; That ye may walk honestly toward them that are without, and that ye may have lack of nothing.
> (1 Thessalonians 4:11-12)

This scripture encourages us that if we walk honestly with our Christian brothers and sisters, we are sure to have strength to do the same with the people who have not yet known the saving grace of God. We must watch our conversation, not just in church but wherever we find ourselves. As we put these seven principles into practice, we will have a greater chance of maintaining a holy lifestyle by the grace of God.

Conclusion

The Lord our God is coming for a glorious Church; a Church without any blemish, a holy Church bought by His blood. Blessed is that Christian who takes all the resources of heaven to please his master by living a life that is truly holy in the eyes of the Almighty. To become holy, we need to hear the word of God, which is made clear to us by the Spirit. To continue to live in holiness, we need to follow the leading of the Holy Spirit, who enables us to be obedient to all that the Lord has told us to do in our lives.

The fruits and the steps to maintaining a holy life are just steps if we don't allow the Holy Spirit to help us. Our holiness is perfected as we walk in fear of God (see 2 Corinthians 7:1). We can only truly walk this path in faith and with a good conscience (see 1 Timothy 1:19). We must maintain a constant state of thanksgiving, for our holiness is only a reflection of His Holiness (see Psalm 30:4) The God we serve delights in holiness;

it is His nature and He is worshipped in the beauty of holiness (see Psalm 29:2).

God calls us holy (see Hebrews 12:14). Let us be true to our name. We are called to be holy because our God is holy and we must be like our maker (see 1 Peter 1:15-16). A good seed brings forth a good fruit; a holy seed gives forth holy fruit. In order to truly serve the Lord, we must be willing to be like Him. His grace gives us all the help we need. All we need to do is pursue holiness and show forth the fruits. If we want to see God's kingdom come, we must obey the call to walk down the Highway of Holiness and commit to the journey.

My heart's cry and my prayer is that you will see the Lord's guiding hands on the highway of holiness, that you will yield to Him, and that you will let Him empower you to live and maintain a holy lifestyle.

Pleasant Word

To order additional copies of this title call:
1-877-421-READ (7323)
or please visit our Web site at
www.pleasantwordbooks.com

If you enjoyed this quality custom-published book,
drop by our Web site for more books and information.

www.winepressgroup.com
"Your partner in custom publishing."

Printed in the United States
109558LV00002B/1-75/P

9 781414 110592